A Guide to
AMERICAN STATES

Connecticut

THE CONSTITUTION STATE

MEDIA ENHANCED BOOKS
AV² BY WEIGL
ADDED VALUE · AUDIO VISUAL

www.av2books.com

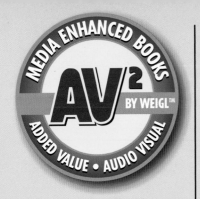

AV² provides enriched content that supplements and complements this book. Weigl's AV² books strive to create inspired learning and engage young minds in a total learning experience.

Your AV² Media Enhanced books come alive with...

Audio
Listen to sections of the book read aloud.

Key Words
Study vocabulary, and complete a matching word activity.

Go to **www.av2books.com**, and enter this book's unique code.

Video
Watch informative video clips.

Quizzes
Test your knowledge.

BOOK CODE

T 1 4 3 3 9

Embedded Weblinks
Gain additional information for research.

Slide Show
View images and captions, and prepare a presentation.

AV² by Weigl brings you media enhanced books that support active learning.

Try This!
Complete activities and hands-on experiments.

... and much, much more!

Published by AV² by Weigl
350 5th Avenue, 59th Floor
New York, NY 10118
Website: www.av2books.com   www.weigl.com

Library of Congress Cataloging-in-Publication Data

Webster, Christine.
 Connecticut / Christine Webster.
    p. cm.
Includes index.
ISBN 978-1-61690-779-2 (hardcover : alk. paper) -- ISBN 978-1-61690-454-8 (online)
1. Connecticut--Juvenile literature. I. Title.
F94.3.W43 2011
974.6--dc23
                          2011018318

Printed in the United States of America in North Mankato, Minnesota

052011
WEP180511

Project Coordinator Jordan McGill
Art Director Terry Paulhus

Photo Credits
Every reasonable effort has been made to trace ownership and to obtain permission to reprint copyright material. The publishers would be pleased to have any errors or omissions brought to their attention so that they may be corrected in subsequent printings.

Weigl acknowledges Getty Images as its primary image supplier for this title.

Contents

Hartford is one of the country's oldest cities. American Indians originally called the area Saukiog. Colonists renamed it in 1637 after Hertford, England.

Introduction

C onnecticut is one of six New England states, located in the northeastern corner of the United States. Despite being the third-smallest state in the country, Connecticut has much to offer. The state is a perfect combination of old and new. It is a place where busy seaports blend into magnificent coastal views and where bustling cities are supported by colonial architecture. In the countryside, autumn leaves provide a vibrant backdrop for the state's many white-steepled churches. Since Connecticut is believed to have the world's first written **constitution**, it is not surprising that its official nickname is the Constitution State.

The birthplace of the hamburger is in Connecticut. Louis' Lunch, a well-known eatery, claims to have made the first hamburger in 1900.

In centuries past many farm families looked forward to visits from people who traveled the countryside selling such items as hats, pins, buttons, rifles, and clocks.

In the 1700s and 1800s Connecticut Yankee **peddlers** traveled across the country with horse-drawn carts that were filled with various items for sale. Some Connecticut Yankee peddlers reportedly sold small, wood-carved "nutmegs" in place of real nutmegs, and so Connecticut also became known as the Nutmeg State.

Connecticut is one of the wealthiest states in the nation. It has the third-highest **median income**. The strength of its economy is a result of the industrial and service sectors as well as its skilled and educated workforce. Factories produce weapons, sewing machines, jet engines, helicopters, motors, hardware, cutlery, and submarines. Growth in finance, insurance, and real estate has contributed to Connecticut's wealth. Today Connecticut combines its strong economy with excellent educational facilities, pleasant living conditions, rich history, vibrant culture, and beautiful scenery.

Where Is Connecticut?

Connecticut's name comes from the Algonquian Indian word *Quinnehtukqut*, which means "land on the long tidal river." The broad Connecticut River flows down the center of the state. Its riverbanks were once home to many American Indians. Early colonists built Connecticut's first towns along the river. Ships carried goods from Hartford to locations around the world. Today Hartford is the state capital.

Connecticut is bordered by the states of Massachusetts, New York, and Rhode Island. It is linked by an extensive highway system. Vehicles can whisk through the state in less than two hours. Connecticut is also within a few hours drive of major cities, such as New York and Boston. Among the major highways is Interstate 95, which runs along Long Island Sound. Interstate 91 heads north from New Haven, all the way through New England and up to Canada. The eastern section of Interstate 84 is known as the Yankee Expressway.

The WWE headquarters is located in Stamford, Connecticut.

Connecticut's many airports help connect it to the rest of the world. Bradley International Airport, located north of Hartford, is the state's major airport. The second-largest airport in New England, Bradley serves more than 5 million travelers each year. The Metro-North Railroad carries thousands of passengers each day to New York City and across Connecticut.

Connecticut's limited natural resources forced colonists to use their creativity to invent new products. In 1790 the United States **Patent** Office opened, and for the next 150 years Connecticut received more patents **per capita** than any other state. Many brands of cigars, clocks, combs, firearms, and hats were made in the state.

I DIDN'T KNOW THAT!

The Constitution State is divided into eight counties.

Connecticut covers more than 4,800 square miles of land.

Although Montana's land area is almost 30 times bigger than Connecticut's, Connecticut has more than four times as many people.

The Metro-North Railroad serves more than 100 commuter stations in southwestern Connecticut as well as parts of New York.

Mapping Connecticut

Connecticut is the southernmost state in New England. Massachusetts is to the north of the state, New York to the west, Long Island Sound to the south, and Rhode Island to the east. Connecticut's three major waterways are the Connecticut, Thames, and Housatonic rivers. The state has about 8,400 miles of rivers and streams.

Sites and Symbols

STATE SEAL
Connecticut

STATE BIRD
American Robin

STATE FLOWER
Mountain Laurel

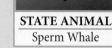

STATE FLAG
Connecticut

STATE ANIMAL
Sperm Whale

STATE TREE
White Oak

Nickname The Constitution State

Motto *Qui Transtulit Sustinet* (He Who Transplanted Still Sustains)

Song "Yankee Doodle"

Entered the Union January 9, 1788, as the 5th state

Capital Hartford

Population (2010 Census) 3,574,097 Ranked 29th state

VERMONT

NEW HAMPSHIRE

NEW YORK

MASSACHUSETTS

CONNECTICUT

RHODE ISLAND

Manchester
Haverhill
Troy
Nashua
Lowell
Greenfield
Chelmsford
Leominster
Pittsfield
Reading
Malden
Amherst
Clinton
Hudson
Somerville
Cambridge
Northampton
Newton
Worcester
Framingham
Boston
Chicopee
Norwood
Westfield
Springfield
Milford
Longmeadow
Webster
Windsor Locks
Pawtucket
Torrington
Windsor
Storrs
Providence*
Attleboro
Hartford
Cranston
East Providence
West Hartford
East Hartford
Warwick
Bristol
Willimantic
Fall River
New Britain
Waterbury
Middletown
Norwich
Meriden
Naugatuck
Wallingford
Danbury
Westerly
New Haven
New London
Groton
West Haven
East Haven
Stratford
Milford
Bridgeport
Norwalk
Stamford
New Rochelle
Atlantic Ocean
Medford
N
Jericho
Plainview
Levittown
Merrick
Map Scale
Long Beach
0   50 Miles

LEGEND
— Road
— River
⭐ State Capital
• City
▮ Connecticut
— State Border

STATE CAPITAL

Connecticut's state capital is Hartford. Connecticut had twin capitals, New Haven and Hartford in 1701. Hartford became the official capital in 1875.

United States

Connecticut

Hawai'i   Alaska

The Land

The Connecticut River divides the Constitution State in half. The Eastern and Western Highlands are on either side of the river. The Central Lowland runs through the center of the state, between the two highlands.

The Eastern Highlands consist of low, thickly forested hills. This fertile area has few elevations over 1,300 feet and is drained by several rivers. Many hills are level and have been cleared and used for agriculture. The state's highest altitudes are found in the Western Highlands. Thick forests cover much of this rugged area.

The Central Lowland is made up of reddish sandstone, shale, and deep, rich soil. It has Connecticut's best farmland.

CONNECTICUT RIVER

The Connecticut River is one of the longest rivers in the United States without a major port or harbor. This is because shifting sandbars at the river's mouth make navigation difficult.

MOUNT FRISSELL

The highest peak in Connecticut is Mount Frissell, which is 2,380 feet tall.

CONNECTICUT RIVER VALLEY

While Connecticut's soil is generally infertile, the Connecticut River valley has rich soils for growing crops.

Connecticut has 30 state forests and 90 state parks. Hammonasset Beach State Park, the state's largest shoreline park, has more than 2 miles of beach along Long Island Sound.

LONG ISLAND SOUND

Connecticut's coastline stretches for 253 miles along Long Island Sound, which is an extension of the Atlantic Ocean.

The majority of Connecticut's woodlands are privately owned.

Winters in Connecticut
are typically snowy.

Climate

C onnecticut has a moderate climate with four distinct seasons. Summer temperatures average 72° Fahrenheit, while the average temperature in the winter is around 26° F. The highest temperature ever recorded in Connecticut was 106° F in Danbury on July 15, 1995. The state's lowest recorded temperature was –37° F in Norfolk on February 16, 1943.

The state receives 35 to 45 inches of snow each year, though northwest Connecticut typically gets nearly twice that amount. The season's first snowfall often takes place by November. Connecticut's snowiest month ever was December 1945, when more than 45 inches fell.

Average Annual Temperature Across Connecticut

The temperatures in the summer and in the winter in Connecticut are usually not extreme. Bridgeport, Middletown, and Hartford have average annual temperatures above 50° Fahrenheit. Why might Norfolk have a lower average annual temperature?

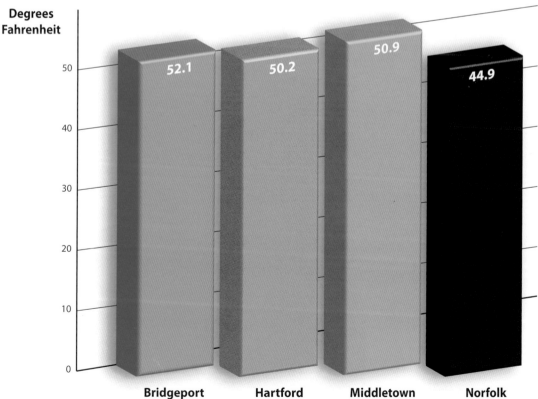

Natural Resources

Water is an important natural resource in Connecticut. It provides habitats for fish and transportation routes for boats. During colonial times, Connecticut's rivers and waterfalls powered many of the state's factories and mills. By the early 21st century, however, hydroelectric plants produced only about 2 percent of Connecticut's electricity.

Commercial fishers in Connecticut harvest fish and other seafood from Long Island Sound and the Atlantic Ocean.

Mining was once important in Connecticut, but most of the copper and iron mines have closed. Sand, gravel, stone, feldspar, mica, and clay are still produced in the state.

Connecticut was once almost entirely covered by trees, but most old forest has since been cut. Through conservation efforts and the decline of the lumber industry, however, forest removal no longer exceeds its growth in Connecticut. Today, woodlands cover nearly two-thirds of the state.

Northern Connecticut is home to birch, beech, maple, and hemlock trees. The state's southern woodlands are mostly oak. Hickory, oak, birch, maple, and ash are valuable to the lumber industry.

One of Connecticut's leading mineral products, gravel is widely used as a building material.

Plants

Connecticut's beautiful scenery is enhanced by its many plants and trees. The most common types of trees include pignut and shagbark hickory, oak, maple, ash, white pine, hemlock, red cedar, and other hardwoods.

Common flowering plants are pink dogwood, wild cherry, and jack-in-the-pulpit. The state flower, the mountain laurel, is noted for its white and pink blossoms. Some consider it the most beautiful flowering shrub in North America.

Connecticut is home to many **endangered** plants, including the balsam fir, Indian paintbrush, white milkweed, hairy lip fern, and goldenseal.

The Connecticut Department of Environmental Protection provides many programs that research and protect Connecticut's natural resources. One important program is the **reforestation** of state land. There are also a number of private organizations that engage in conservation efforts.

PIGNUT HICKORY TREE

Pignut hickory trees have short branches and produce thick-shelled nuts. Early settlers made brooms from strips of the wood.

PINK DOGWOOD TREE

The spectacular dogwood tree flowers with long-lasting spring blooms. The trees grow to heights of 40 feet.

JACK-IN-THE-PULPITS

Jack-in-the-pulpits have one or two large leaves that rise on their own stems. They can grow to be one to three feet tall.

INDIAN PAINTBRUSHES

This endangered plant can reach 6 to 16 inches high. The stems form clumps topped by long red spikes that resemble paintbrushes.

The white oak became the official state tree in 1947 in remembrance of the historic **Charter Oak**. In 1662 Connecticut received a charter from King Charles II of England, which established the area as an independent colony. Twenty-five years later, King James II sent officials to retrieve the charter. A captain named Joseph Wadsworth hid the charter in an ancient hollow oak tree called the Charter Oak, which was knocked over by a storm in 1856. The Charter Oak is featured on the Connecticut quarter, released by the U.S. Mint in 1999.

American Indians used the bark from birch trees to make canoes.

Animals

Millions of years ago, dinosaurs were inhabitants of Connecticut. The state fossil, *Eubrontes giganteus*, is a track made by a three-toed dinosaur. By the time the first European settlers arrived, different kinds of animal life existed. Many deer, wolves, and smaller animals, such as porcupines and foxes, occupied the land. Humans have forced out most of the large animals, such as panthers and bears. Today, rabbits, beavers, minks, squirrels, and raccoons inhabit Connecticut. While most birds migrate each year, blue jays, chickadees, and English sparrows live in the state year-round. Snowy owls have also been seen in Connecticut.

Connecticut's many streams and lakes are stocked with bass, perch, pickerel, and trout. Oysters, lobsters, and crabs are found in the coastal waters. The Fisheries Division of the Connecticut Department of Environmental Protection manages Connecticut's fish supply. It keeps a close watch on fish and endangered species. The fish populations are increasing as a result.

SNOWY OWL

Snowy owls sometimes come southward to Connecticut in the middle of winter. Unlike other owls, snowy owls hunt during the day and night.

RED FOX

The red fox, a member of the dog family, lives across Connecticut.

RABBIT

Rabbits live all over the state. They can weigh almost 3 pounds. These small mammals feed on grasses in the summer and bark, twigs, and tree buds in the winter.

BLUE JAY

The blue jay has a handsome crest of bright blue, mostly blue feathers, and a white breast and face. Native to North America, this bird is common in Connecticut.

The sperm whale became Connecticut's official state animal in 1975. In past centuries, Connecticut whaling ships hunted and killed sperm whales, and their oil was used in lamps and other products. Today, the sperm whale is an endangered species.

When settlers first arrived in Connecticut, wild turkeys were common. Harsh weather, hunting, and the clearing of forests caused the wild turkeys to disappear by the early 1800s. In the 1970s, wildlife biologists released wild turkeys in the area. Today, there are about 40,000 wild turkeys throughout the state.

Tourism

Connecticut's rustic landscape, beaches, and busy harbors attract millions of visitors each year. Connecticut also offers tourists a glimpse of history. Visitors can take a step back in time as they walk through an old seaport. Situated on some 40 acres along the Mystic River, Mystic Seaport: The Museum of America and the Sea has a fully restored shipyard. Other features include the last wooden whaleboat in the United States, a planetarium, a research library, and one of the largest collections of maritime photographs in the world. Mystic Seaport attracts more than 1 million visitors each year.

The Barnum Museum in Bridgeport is a popular destination for circus fans. The museum is a celebration of the life of Connecticut-born P. T. Barnum, creator of the circus known as "The Greatest Show on Earth."

MYSTIC SEAPORT

Mystic Seaport offers a rare portrait of maritime life. Visitors can tour a re-created seaport village and board an early 19th-century whaling ship to see how sailors lived more than 100 years ago.

BARNUM MUSEUM

Visitors to the Barnum Museum can learn about the 25-inch, 15-pound man known as Tom Thumb as well as Jumbo, the 6½-ton African bull elephant.

PEABODY MUSEUM

The Peabody Museum of Natural History at Yale University is home to many fascinating exhibits. The museum features an Egyptian mummy, a life-size bronze statue of the dinosaur *Torosaurus latus*, and a series of skeletons showing the evolution of humans.

MARITIME AQUARIUM AT NORWALK

Children can learn about the marine life of Long Island Sound at the Maritime Aquarium at Norwalk. Visitors can take a close look at oysters, seahorses, lobsters, and other small creatures or stare into the eyes of a 9-foot shark. Displayed in a 110,000-gallon open ocean tank are sharks, bluefish, and rays.

Gillette Castle stands on a hill high above the Connecticut River. Designed by actor William Gillette, the castle is one of Connecticut's favorite attractions.

Nature lovers can still hike many trails originally cut by American Indians.

Connecticut's farming communities honor their rich history with agricultural fairs held throughout the state. The fairs showcase a variety of farm goods, from home-grown vegetables to beautiful needlework.

The Discovery Museum in Bridgeport has many hands-on exhibits, a planetarium, and computer-simulated space missions.

The Connecticut Science Center in Hartford opened in 2009. It features 150 hands-on exhibits, a state-of-the-art 3D digital theater, and four educational labs.

Industry

C onnecticut's economy has changed through the years. While most of the early settlers were farmers, the number of farmers began to decline with the rise of manufacturing in the 1800s. Many farmers went to work in factories, and manufacturing became the foundation of the state's economy. In the late 20th century the economy shifted again, as traditional manufacturing activities gave way to new high-technology industries. Service industries such as insurance and health care also became increasingly important.

Industries in Connecticut
Value of Goods and Services in Millions of Dollars

Manufacturing is an important part of Connecticut's economy. So are many industries in which workers help, or provide a service for, other people. Why might the health care industry be as large as it is?

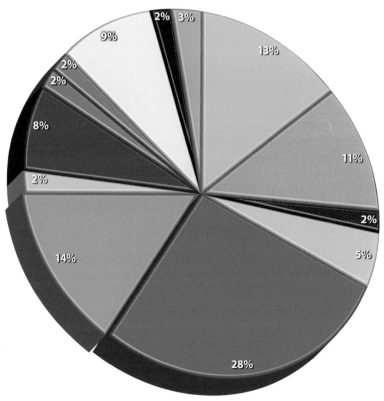

LEGEND

✳	Agriculture, Forestry, and Fishing	$371
✳	Mining	$104
■	Utilities	$4,256
■	Construction	$5,793
■	Manufacturing	$28,864
■	Wholesale and Retail Trade	$23,169
■	Transportation	$3,666
■	Media and Entertainment	$10,284
■	Finance, Insurance, and Real Estate	$61,023
■	Professional and Technical Services	$29,282
■	Education	$3,480
■	Health Care	$17,024
■	Hotels and Restaurants	$4,126
■	Other Services	$4,285
■	Government	$20,448

TOTAL $216,175

*Less than 1%. Percentages may not add to 100 because of rounding.

Shellfish were once abundant in the coastal waters of Connecticut. In the late 1800s the annual catch began declining because of pollution. Nevertheless, commercial fishers still catch approximately 8,000 tons of seafood each year, including flounder, cod, and lobster.

Connecticut is a significant source of tobacco. The state produces high-quality broadleaf tobacco, which is used mainly to make cigar wrappers. It is grown under a permanent cover of open-mesh cloth that is held up by poles. The mesh protects the tobacco from direct sunlight and heavy rain.

Commercial fishing boats from Connecticut harvest clams, oysters, and lobsters.

First published in 1764, *The Hartford Courant* is the oldest continuously published newspaper in the United States. Thomas Green started the paper as a weekly and kept it going by selling clothing, hardware, and stationery out of the store in front of his office.

The dramatic decline in farms in the state led to the passage of a farm preservation act in 1978. Today, Connecticut farms produce dairy products, eggs, fruits, vegetables, tobacco, and **nursery** stock.

More than one-third of the state's workforce is employed in the service industry. Service positions include nurses, teachers, and store clerks.

Goods and Services

Connecticut's limited natural resources forced its citizens to develop new ways of making money. Creative citizens have developed many important inventions, such as firearms, submarines, and corkscrews. In the early 1800s Seth Thomas pioneered the mass production of clocks and founded the Seth Thomas Clock Company. In 1839 Charles Goodyear, who was born in Connecticut, first created **vulcanized rubber**.

Manufacturing is an important part of Connecticut's economy. Jet aircraft engines, computer equipment, and transportation equipment are manufactured in the state. Pez candy and Lego toys are also made in Connecticut. The state's principal manufacturing centers are Hartford, Bridgeport, New Haven, and Danbury.

In 1839 Charles Goodyear accidentally dropped a mixture of rubber and sulfur onto a hot stove. The rubber, instead of melting, became strong and elastic. Although he was granted a patent on his vulcanized rubber, Goodyear never profited financially from his important invention.

The insurance industry, along with financial services and real estate, is a very important part of Connecticut's economy. The insurance industry was created in the 1700s for merchants who were concerned about losing their ships and cargo to pirates and accidents. There soon came a need for fire insurance, and in 1810 the Hartford Fire Insurance Group was formed. It is one of the nation's oldest insurance companies and still operates in Hartford. It is now part of The Hartford Financial Services Group, Inc. Hartford is known as the Insurance Capital of the World.

Education has always been important in Connecticut. The state's first public school opened in 1641 in New Haven. Several notable postsecondary schools can be found in Connecticut. The oldest and best-known university in the state is Yale University. It was founded in 1701 in New Haven. Other notable postsecondary schools are the University of Connecticut, Trinity College, and the University of Hartford.

Yale University is the third-oldest university in the United States.

There are more than 100 insurance companies in Connecticut, which is sometimes called the Insurance State.

In 1650 a law was passed requiring every town with more than 50 families to establish an elementary school. Those towns with more than 100 families had to provide a secondary school as well.

Connecticut has approximately 195 public libraries. The largest and most important library collection is held at the Yale University Library.

American Indians

For thousands of years before the first settlers arrived, American Indians were living in the Connecticut area. By the 1600s there were between 6,000 and 7,000 American Indians. They belonged to several Algonquian-speaking groups. The most powerful of these were the Pequot. Other groups included the Mohegan, Nipmuc, and Niantic. The American Indians cut trails through the dense forests to travel between their villages. They hunted animals and gathered wild berries for food. They also fished in the streams and grew beans, corn, and squash. The American Indians often traveled with the seasons to take advantage of the natural resources. They built **wigwams** and **longhouses** from saplings and used bark and branches to cover them.

Samson Occum, born in Connecticut in 1723, was a widely admired Mohegan writer, spiritual leader, and teacher. He wrote and spoke English.

Although relations between Europeans and American Indians were friendly at first, tensions grew as more settlers arrived in Connecticut. This led to the first major war of New England—the Pequot War of 1637. The colonists formed alliances with the Mohegan and the Narragansett (from Rhode Island) and led a surprise attack on the Pequot, destroying their fort at Mystic. The remaining Pequot were captured and sold into slavery or held under the control of other American Indian groups. The surviving Pequot became known as the Mashantucket Pequot.

The Pequot War of 1637 ended in large losses of life. It was the first major conflict between American Indians and white settlers in New England.

A clergyman from England named Thomas Hooker led a group of settlers to what is now Connecticut in 1636.

Explorers

Dutch explorer Adriaen Block sailed up the Connecticut River and along the coast in 1614. He was the first European to reach Connecticut. American Indians greeted him in peace. Block sent reports back to Europe of the land's beauty and trade possibilities. In 1633 the Dutch set up a small trading fort at the end of the navigable portion of the Connecticut River, near the present site of Hartford. It was called Fort Good Hope. The Dutch soon became trading partners with the American Indians.

Settlers from nearby Massachusetts were also exploring the fertile Connecticut River Valley. They had originally left their homes in Great Britain in search of political and religious freedom. In the 1630s these settlers began establishing posts in what is now Connecticut. Windsor was founded in 1633, and Wethersfield was established in 1634. In 1636 a group led by the Reverend Thomas Hooker formed a colony at Hartford. The English settlements grew steadily, and by the mid-1650s the Dutch had left the area.

Timeline of Settlement

Early Exploration

1614 The first European comes to what is now Connecticut. Dutch explorer Adriaen Block sails up the Connecticut River.

First Settlements

1633 The Dutch establish a trading fort near what is now Hartford.

1636 Reverend Thomas Hooker founds a colony at Hartford.

1637 English colonists fight the Pequot Indians in the Pequot War.

1639 After forming a single colony in the late 1690s, the Hartford, Windsor, and Wethersfield settlements adopt the Fundamental Orders on January 14. This document establishes a government for the colony and later serves as a model for the U.S. Constitution.

Royal Colony

1662 Connecticut receives a charter from King Charles II of England, which establishes the area as a royal colony.

American Revolution and After

1775–1783 The American Revolution ends in the creation of the United States.

1788 After much debate, which included political cartoons depicting the state as a wagon stuck in mud, Connecticut ratifies, or approves, the new U.S. Constitution and becomes the fifth state to enter the Union.

1848 Connecticut outlaws slavery, giving all African American residents their freedom.

Early Settlers

T he state's earliest colonists were farmers. They raised only enough food for their own needs. These early settlers grew vegetables and grains and kept a few animals. They made their own clothing, tools, and weapons. The forests provided the colonists with wood for fuel and for construction.

Map of Settlements and Resources in Early Connecticut

4 Connecticut's beaver population helped fuel the Dutch fur trade in the early 1600s.

1 The Dutch were the first European settlers in what is now Connecticut. In 1633, they founded a trading fort near what is now Hartford. It was called Good Hope.

2 In 1638, a group of English settlers founded the New Haven Colony on Long Island Sound. It became part of the colony of Connecticut in 1662.

5 With a lack of many natural resources, Connecticut and its ocean waters have always provided a reliable source of seafood to the population.

6 In the 1600s, settlers came to the Connecticut River Valley to farm its fertile soil.

3 Reverend Thomas Hooker from Massachusetts established a settlement in what is now Hartford in 1636. He believed citizens should be allowed to choose their own leaders. Hooker is sometimes called the Father of American Democracy.

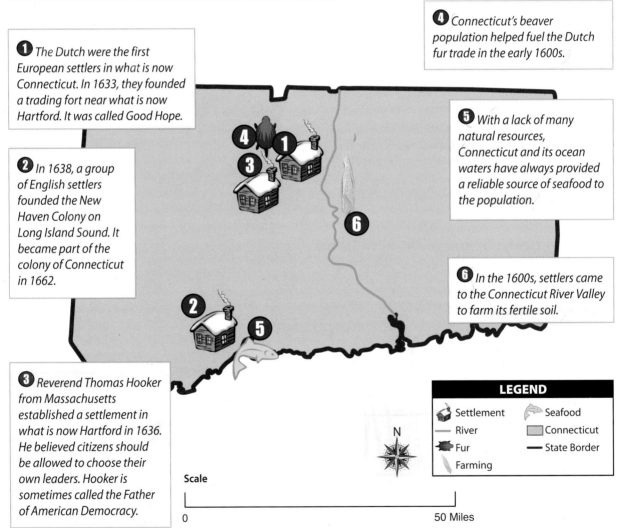

LEGEND

Settlement		Seafood	
River		Connecticut	
Fur		State Border	
Farming			

N

Scale

0   50 Miles

In the late 1630s the settlements of Hartford, Windsor, and Wethersfield decided to join together to form a single colony. The colonists created their own set of laws. This document, known as the Fundamental Orders, was adopted on January 14, 1639. Considered to be the world's first written constitution, it established a government that included a legislature and court system. It also called for elections, and John Haynes was elected the colony's first governor.

The first European settlers in what is now Connecticut in the 1600s were from Holland and England. They sometimes had conflicts, and as a result, the Dutch abandoned the area by mid-century.

From 1790 until 1840 Connecticut's population increased by between 4 and 8 percent every 10 years.

In 1790 the population of Connecticut was 237,946 people. This was approximately 6 percent of the total population of the United States. While most of the citizens were of European heritage, Connecticut was also home to many slaves.

In the 1840s many Irish people came to Connecticut to escape the Great Potato Famine in Ireland. The 1900s brought a wave of **immigration**. Germans, French, and Canadians came to Connecticut because of the state's growing demand for labor. They were followed by people from Italy, Sweden, Norway, and Poland. In the late 20th century the state saw a rise in immigrants from China and India.

Notable People

Many notable Connecticut residents have contributed to the development of their state and their country. They have devoted their lives to improving the world around them. The Constitution State has produced war heroes, committed educators, inventors in the areas of industry and medicine, beloved authors, and groundbreaking political leaders.

**NATHAN HALE
(1755–1776)**

Born in Coventry in northeast Connecticut, Hale was a schoolteacher who then served as an officer in the American Revolution. He became a spy for General George Washington in 1776. He was caught by British soldiers on September 21, 1776, and hanged without trial the next day. He was 21 years old. Hale's last words reportedly were "I only regret that I have but one life to lose for my country."

**NOAH WEBSTER
(1758–1843)**

Born in West Hartford, Webster began writing his *American Dictionary of the English Language* in 1807. Finished in 1828, it became the standard dictionary of American English.

ELI WHITNEY (1765–1825)

After graduating from Yale University, Whitney traveled to the South and saw cotton farmers struggling to separate the fibers from the seeds. He invented the cotton gin to clean the seeds off cotton quickly. But Whitney's most important contribution to technology may have been developing a way to mass produce interchangeable parts. Whitney built a very successful gun factory that used this system in New Haven.

HARRIET BEECHER STOWE (1811–1896)

Stowe, the daughter of a minister, was born in Litchfield. She worked as a schoolteacher in Hartford and Cincinnati, Ohio, where she learned about slave life in nearby Kentucky. She drew on the experience to write the antislavery novel *Uncle Tom's Cabin*, published in 1852.

CARRIE SAXON PERRY (1931–)

A native of Hartford, Carrie Saxon Perry became mayor of her hometown city in 1987. She was the first African American woman to be elected mayor of a large city in the United States. Often seen wearing one of her signature hats, Perry worked as a social worker before she took office.

I DIDN'T KNOW THAT!

Ella T. Grasso (1919–1981) became the first woman to serve as governor of Connecticut in 1975. A Democrat, Grasso was also the first woman to be elected governor of a state in her own right, without being preceded in office by her husband. She died of cancer in Hartford in 1981.

Robert K. Jarvik (1946–), from Stamford, invented the world's first artificial heart in 1982. Researchers continue to work on developing an improved artificial heart.

Population

onnecticut has almost 738 people for every square mile, making it one of the country's most densely populated states. Most of its residents live in urban areas. The largest cities in Connecticut are Bridgeport, Hartford, New Haven, Stamford, and Waterbury. Small and sparsely populated towns still exist in the countryside. Approximately 9,600 American Indians live in Connecticut, and there are a number of reservations throughout the state. Two large Pequot reservations can be found in Ledyard Town and North Stonington. Colchester is the site of a 106-acre reservation. A few American Indians live on the Schaghticoke reservation in Kent. A Mohegan reservation is located at Uncasville.

Connecticut Population 1950–2010

Connecticut's population has grown every decade since 1950, but in most recent decades, growth has been slow. What factors may make the population of some states increase more rapidly or slowly than others?

Number of People

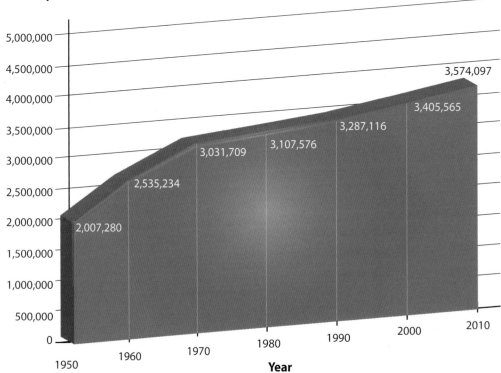

New Haven is the third-largest city in Connecticut by population.

Bridgeport is the largest city in Connecticut. It has a population of more than 137,000 citizens.

More than 350,000 African Americans reside in Connecticut. Most live in the state's five largest cities. More than 30 percent of the populations of New Haven and Hartford are African American.

Trumbull is home to a tiny American Indian reservation about one city block in size.

Bridgeport is Connecticut's most populous city. Since the 1950s, however, the city has lost residents every decade. Some people have moved away to find job opportunities elsewhere.

Politics and Government

C onnecticut's earliest settlers are believed to have created the first constitution. Today, the state is governed under its fourth constitution, which was adopted in 1965.

Connecticut has three branches of government. The governor, who is elected by the people to a four-year term, heads the executive branch.

The legislative branch consists of a bicameral, or two-house, legislature. It has a 36-member Senate and a 151-member House of Representatives. Members of each house are elected to two-year terms. The legislative branch is responsible for making the laws of Connecticut.

The Connecticut State Capitol, constructed out of marble and granite, was completed in 1879. It cost $2.5 million to build.

State senators meet in the State Senate Chamber in Hartford's Connecticut State Capitol.

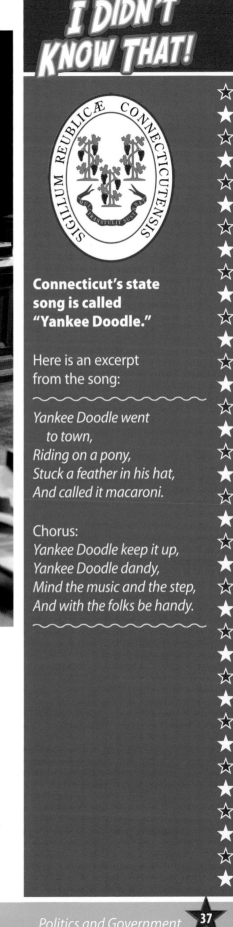
The judicial branch interprets the law and administers justice. The state's highest court, the Supreme Court, handles the appeals of those dissatisfied with the lower courts' rulings.

Local governments in Connecticut provide education, police and fire protection, and other services. Most larger communities have an elected mayor and council. Some smaller communities have elected mayors, and others have town or city managers.

Cultural Groups

While most residents of Connecticut were born in the United States, they can trace their roots to ancestors from all over the world. Approximately 80 percent of the population is of European heritage. Within this group, Italian Americans are among the most numerous. Italian Americans are proud of their culture and love to demonstrate this each summer during the Festival Italiano. The festival is held in Westport every July and features Italian foods, arts, and crafts. Festivalgoers have the opportunity to sample some of the best pizza Connecticut has to offer. The event, which opens with a large parade, is sponsored by the Sons of Italy, and the money raised goes to charities.

Almost 20 percent of Connecticut's residents have Italian ancestry. Cultural events, parades, and restaurants celebrate Italian heritage in the state.

American Indians in Connecticut celebrate their culture each year. The Mashantucket Pequot Tribal Nation puts on festivals that showcase the group's traditions. One such festival is the annual Feast of Green Corn and Dance, called the Schemitzun. The event, which runs for several days, is noted for its dance and drum competitions. Visitors can also buy arts and crafts from American Indian vendors and watch demonstrations of basket weaving. The Mashantucket Pequot also operate Foxwoods Resort Casino, the world's largest casino complex. It takes in more than $1 billion each year.

Many other cultural festivals are held in the summer and the fall of each year. The Connecticut Scottish Festival in Goshen features bagpipe players and dance competitions each October. North Haven hosts the Connecticut Irish Festival, which includes sporting events, an agricultural fair, and musical performances. While some food festivals serve traditional New England food, many have added rich flavors from China, Ireland, Italy, Mexico, and Puerto Rico. Many ethnic restaurants can be found throughout Connecticut.

The population in Connecticut is diverse. The state is home to many Asian families.

Roman Catholics are the largest religious group in Connecticut.

More than 630,000 people in Connecticut are of Italian descent.

Under a 1993 agreement, the Mashantucket Pequot pay Connecticut one quarter of the money they earn from their casino's slot machines. The state puts this money into social programs.

New Haven hosts an annual St. Patrick's Day parade. People dress up in green, listen to live Irish music, and watch dancers do jigs. The parade attracts thousands of spectators.

Arts and Entertainment

Many well-known entertainers and artists are connected to the Constitution State. Actor Paul Newman studied at the Yale School of Drama in New Haven and later settled in the state. He starred in numerous movies and even owned a food company, Newman's Own, which donates its profits to charitable causes. Movie star Katharine Hepburn was born in Connecticut. She won four Academy Awards for best actress throughout her impressive career. Actor Glenn Close, who was born in Greenwich, appeared in *101 Dalmatians*, playing the evil Cruella De Vil. Children's author and illustrator Maurice Sendak has called Connecticut home. Sendak wrote and illustrated the popular children's book *Where the Wild Things Are*.

One of Connecticut's most-treasured theaters is the Long Wharf Theater in New Haven. Many plays are performed here before moving to larger audiences in New York City. The Shubert Performing Arts Center in New Haven is considered to be Connecticut's center for cultural life. In addition to theater, the center offers opera, dance, and music performances.

Author and illustrator Maurice Sendak published Where the Wild Things Are *in 1964, and millions of children have enjoyed it ever since. A popular movie based on the book came out in 2009.*

One of the best places in the world to see real dinosaur tracks is at Dinosaur State Park. Dinosaur tracks were discovered in Rocky Hill in 1966. Since then, more than 2,000 tracks have been uncovered. The tracks range in length from 10 inches to 16 inches and are 3½ feet to 4½ feet apart. The 200-million-year-old tracks are housed under a giant dome. Visitors can make plaster molds of dinosaur footprints.

Each summer Music Mountain hosts the oldest continuous summer chamber music festival in the United States. First held in 1930, the festival features string quartets, piano recitals, and jazz concerts. In June residents can watch the Northwest Connecticut Balloon Festival and Craft Fair in Goshen. Hot-air balloons are launched into the sky, while spectators on the ground are provided with entertainment.

Singer, songwriter, and guitarist John Mayer was born in Bridgeport in 1977. He has won several Grammy Awards for his alternative rock. He has performed with various musicians, including rapper Kanye West, bluesman B. B. King, and country-pop singer Taylor Swift.

John Mayer began playing guitar when he was 13 years old and released his own debut album at the age of 21. By 26, he had won his first Grammy Award.

I DIDN'T KNOW THAT!

The 1662 charter and the Fundamental Orders are on display at the Connecticut State Library in Hartford.

The author Mark Twain had a home in Hartford. It was there that he wrote *The Adventures of Tom Sawyer*, *The Adventures of Huckleberry Finn*, and *The Prince and the Pauper*.

The popular play *A Streetcar Named Desire* made its debut at the Shubert Performing Arts Center in 1947.

Many well-known entertainers have had homes in Connecticut, including talk-show host David Letterman and actor Tom Cruise.

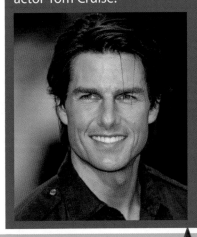

Sports

Connecticut's many forested hills and valleys invite hikers and horseback riders. The Appalachian Trail, which cuts through northwest Connecticut, is a perfect trek. The streams, lakes, and coastal waters of the state have popular areas for swimming, boating, camping, or fishing. Fly-fishing is a popular sport in Connecticut.

In the winter skiers gather at the many hilltops and ski resorts. Mohawk Mountain, a very popular place to ski, is Connecticut's oldest and largest ski area. Other winter activities include iceboating and ice-skating.

With its numerous caves and caverns, Connecticut is also popular with spelunkers. Spelunkers are people who explore caves. They have to wear warm clothing and a helmet. They also use light sources, such as flashlights, to see fascinating rock formations or glimpses of animals such as bats.

Downhill and cross-country skiing, ice fishing, and hockey are popular winter activities in Connecticut.

College sports are played all over the state and attract many fans. The University of Connecticut's men's and women's basketball team, the Connecticut Huskies, have many supporters. The school has produced a number of standout players, including Rebecca Lobo, who was named the best female college basketball player in the Final Four tournament in 1995 and won a gold medal at the 1996 Olympic Games. In 2004 the University of Connecticut became the first school in National Collegiate Athletic Association (NCAA) Division I history to win both the men's and the women's basketball championships.

In 2003 the state's first professional women's basketball team, the Connecticut Sun, began play. Part of the Women's National Basketball Association (WNBA), the team plays at the Mohegan Sun Arena.

Center Tina Charles helped the University of Connecticut win national championships in 2009 and 2010. The Connecticut Sun selected her first overall in the 2010 Women's National Basketball Association Draft.

National Averages Comparison

T he United States is a federal republic, consisting of fifty states and the District of Columbia. Alaska and Hawai'i are the only non-contiguous, or non-touching, states in the nation. Today, the United States of America is the third-largest country in the world in population. The United States Census Bureau takes a census, or count of all the people, every ten years. It also regularly collects other kinds of data about the population and the economy. How does Connecticut compare with the national average?

Comparison Chart

United States 2010 Census Data *	USA	Connecticut
Admission to Union	NA	January 9, 1788
Land Area (in square miles)	3,537,438.44	4,844.80
Population Total	308,745,538	3,574,097
Population Density (people per square mile)	87.28	737.72
Population Percentage Change (April 1, 2000, to April 1, 2010)	9.7%	4.9%
White Persons (percent)	72.4%	77.6%
Black Persons (percent)	12.6%	10.1%
American Indian and Alaska Native Persons (percent)	0.9%	0.3%
Asian Persons (percent)	4.8%	3.8%
Native Hawaiian and Other Pacific Islander Persons (percent)	0.2%	—
Some Other Race (percent)	6.2%	5.6%
Persons Reporting Two or More Races (percent)	2.9%	2.6%
Persons of Hispanic or Latino Origin (percent)	16.3%	13.4%
Not of Hispanic or Latino Origin (percent)	83.7%	86.6%
Median Household Income	$52,029	$68,294
Percentage of People Age 25 or Over Who Have Graduated from High School	80.4%	84.0%

*All figures are based on the 2010 United States Census, with the exception of the last two items.

How to Improve My Community

Strong communities make strong states. Think about what features are important in your community. What do you value? Education? Health? Forests? Safety? Beautiful spaces? Government works to help citizens create ideal living conditions that are fair to all by providing services in communities. Consider what changes you could make in your community. How would they improve your state as a whole? Using this concept web as a guide, write a report that outlines the features you think are most important in your community and what improvements could be made. A strong state needs strong communities.

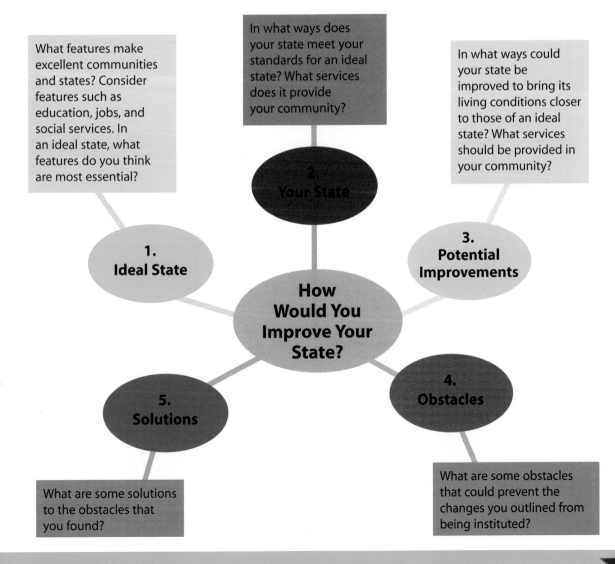

What features make excellent communities and states? Consider features such as education, jobs, and social services. In an ideal state, what features do you think are most essential?

In what ways does your state meet your standards for an ideal state? What services does it provide your community?

In what ways could your state be improved to bring its living conditions closer to those of an ideal state? What services should be provided in your community?

2. Your State

1. Ideal State

3. Potential Improvements

How Would You Improve Your State?

5. Solutions

4. Obstacles

What are some solutions to the obstacles that you found?

What are some obstacles that could prevent the changes you outlined from being instituted?

Exercise Your Mind!

Think about these questions and then use your research skills to find the answers and learn more fascinating facts about Connecticut. A teacher, librarian, or parent may be able to help you locate the best sources to use in your research.

 1 True or False: Connecticut's state shellfish is the lobster.

2 When working as a spy, Nathan Hale disguised himself as a

a. priest
b. schoolmaster
c. doctor
d. lawyer

3 In 1901, Connecticut passed the first automobile law. What was the speed limit the law set?

a. 10 miles per hour
b. 12 miles per hour
c. 20 miles per hour

4 Who received the first patent ever issued to a woman in the United States?

 **5** Which of these products was invented in Connecticut?

a. frisbee
b. tape measure
c. friction matches
d. nuts and bolts
e. all of the above

 6 True or False: The Connecticut River is the longest river in New England.

 7 True or False: In 1793, Eli Whitney invented the first nuclear submarine.

 8 Who was Connecticut's first third-party governor since the Civil War?

a. Jeb Bush
b. George E. Pataki
c. Lowell P. Weicker Jr.
d. John G. Rowland

Words to Know

charter: a written document such as one establishing a colony

constitution: the laws and principles under which a government runs a state or country

endangered: in danger of becoming extinct

immigration: the arrival of people in a new country

longhouses: long, one-room dwellings where several American Indian families lived together

median income: the income level that half the members of a group earn more than and half earn less than

nursery: a place where young trees or other plants are raised for transplanting, for sale, or for study

patent: an exclusive right granted by the government to an inventor

peddlers: people who travel from place to place selling goods

per capita: per person, as in an average

reforestation: the planting of trees in a region that has been logged

vulcanized rubber: rubber treated with sulfur and heat to give it strength

wigwams: round American Indian homes formed by poles and covered in bark

Index

Log on to www.av2books.com

AV² by Weigl brings you media enhanced books that support active learning. Go to www.av2books.com, and enter the special code found on page 2 of this book. You will gain access to enriched and enhanced content that supplements and complements this book. Content includes video, audio, web links, quizzes, a slide show, and activities.

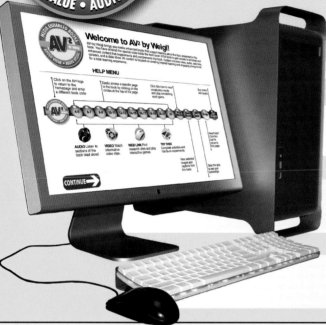

Audio
Listen to sections of the book read aloud.

Video
Watch informative video clips.

Embedded Weblinks
Gain additional information for research.

Try This!
Complete activities and hands-on experiments.

WHAT'S ONLINE?

Try This!	Embedded Weblinks	Video	EXTRA FEATURES
Test your knowledge of the state in a mapping activity.	Discover more attractions in Connecticut.	Watch a video introduction to Connecticut.	**Audio** Listen to sections of the book read aloud.
Find out more about precipitation in your city.	Learn more about the history of the state.	Watch a video about the features of the state.	
Plan what attractions you would like to visit in the state.	Learn the full lyrics of the state song.		**Key Words** Study vocabulary, and complete a matching word activity.
Learn more about the early natural resources of the state.			
Write a biography about a notable resident of Connecticut.			**Slide Show** View images and captions, and prepare a presentation.
Complete an educational census activity.			
			Quizzes Test your knowledge.

AV² was built to bridge the gap between print and digital. We encourage you to tell us what you like and what you want to see in the future.

Sign up to be an AV² Ambassador at www.av2books.com/ambassador.